Original title:
A House of Stories

Copyright © 2025 Creative Arts Management OÜ
All rights reserved.

Author: Alexander Thornton
ISBN HARDBACK: 978-1-80587-095-1
ISBN PAPERBACK: 978-1-80587-565-9

Sketches of Light and Shadow

In the attic, dust bunnies waltz,
They plot schemes, decide who's at fault.
A cat's shadow creeps on the wall,
While the old clock ticks, reminding all.

The broom whispers tales of past fights,
It knows secrets of wild, wobbly nights.
Paint cans grumble of colors gone mad,
As laughter echoes from the room we once had.

Underneath the Painted Skies

Here lies a unicorn, drawn with chalk,
It claims it can dance, but only just squawk.
A roller skated chair, gliding with flair,
Mocks the pot plants; they show no despair.

The sun has a hat made of cheese and bread,
While clouds toss pancakes—good enough to spread.
Jelly-bean rain lands in whimsical spots,
A predictable dance with unpredictable plots.

Fabric of Dreams Sewn Together

A quilt stitched with tales of the odd and bizarre,
Contains pockets of laughter and dreams from afar.
The threads are all tangled, they twist and they twine,
Stitching up fables, both yours and then mine.

The pillowcase hides gnomes that sing at the moon,
While curtains take turns to hum silly tunes.
Buttons once lost are now heroes in flight,
Escaping the laundry in a dazzling light.

The Library of Lost Journeys

Books with mustaches dance off the shelf,
Chasing down stories like elves chasing self.
A bookworm debates with a wise old tome,
"Who knew adventures could feel like a home?"

Pages flutter wildly, and stories conspire,
As plots make toast, and characters tire.
Footnotes giggle in the margins so small,
Whispering secrets that might baffle us all.

Fragments of the Past

Cracked frames hold mischief tight,
Old socks dance under the moonlight.
Loud laughter spills from the walls,
As echoes of ghosts throw silly brawls.

Recipes lost, but the flour still flies,
A kitchen ghost with pie in her eyes.
The chairs creak out jokes you might think,
While dust bunnies plot over glasses of ink.

Timeless Whispers in Dusty Spaces

Around corners, giggles hide,
Beneath the bed, dreams collide.
Old toys plot a grand escape,
While tiny monsters take their shape.

Books stacked high, secrets unfold,
Each spine a tale, precarious and bold.
Whispers crash like waves on the shore,
In every corner, stories galore.

The Windows into Yesterday

Frames that frame those who peek,
A tableau of laughter, a whiff of sneak.
Curtains sway like a dance on cue,
While curtains collect the dust of blue.

Outsiders gaze with puzzled looks,
Seeing paws and fairy books.
The panes filter giggles in whispers sweet,
As heartbeats in sunlight skip a beat.

The Heartbeats of Hidden Rooms

Behind closed doors, secrets tarry,
An old cat declares they're quite merry.
The closet sings with fashion woes,
While socks argue over who knows who best.

A chair spins as if it's keen,
To join the fun of unseen scenes.
In shadows, voices rise and play,
A gallery of smiles at the end of the day.

Beneath the Surface of Silence

In corners where dust bunnies play,
A sock sings a tale of a lonely day.
The cat, with a wink, gives it a nudge,
While the fish in the bowl pretends not to judge.

Whispers of laughter seep through the wall,
As the fridge hums a tune, quite witty and tall.
The chair creaks a joke about life on the run,
In a language that only the curtains have fun.

Rooms of Memory

Each room holds a giggle, a dance, or a chase,
With shadows of socks finding their place.
The mirror's reflection can't stop cracking jokes,
While the couch hosts debates among old-time folks.

In the attic, the dust tells stories untold,
Of pickles on pizza and garlic so bold.
The clock keeps on laughing, though time seems to freeze,

Spinning tales of the past with a tick and a tease.

Chronicles in the Shadows

Beneath the stairs lurks a shy little ghost,
Who sneezes at dust and craves buttered toast.
The shadows wag fingers at things they've delayed,
While giggling at all of the pranks they once played.

A broom stands by, plotting a sweep of its own,
With bristles that tickle, they giggle and moan.
A light flickers softly, igniting the fun,
As the walls join in laughter, 'Oh, what have we done?'

Tales from the Worn Staircase

Each step has a story of slips and of trips,
As the handrail chuckles at old scraped-up hips.
With creaks it composes a symphony grand,
While dust motes waltz like they've had too much sand.

The landing holds memories of snowball fights,
Where pillows were launched in the dim, cozy nights.
So if you should stumble, just laugh it away,
For the staircase is ready to brighten your day.

Corners of Time's Embrace

In the corner sits a chair,
With a parrot who wants to share.
Old tales of clumsy cats,
And shoes that chased the hats.

A clock that ticks in rhyme,
Whispers of forgotten time.
It giggles when the sun
Catches shadows just for fun.

A hat that flies on walls,
And laughter that softly calls.
Grandma hides behind the door,
Pretending she's a dinosaur.

Each creak a comic line,
As stories twist and entwine.
A game of hide and seek,
Where shadows play hide and peek.

The Diary Beneath the Dust

Beneath the old and dusty shelf,
Lies a diary filled with stealth.
Stories of a shoe that danced,
In a sock, it lost its chance.

Each page a slip of giggles,
Tales of cakes that came with wiggles.
It speaks of socks with holes,
And spoons that tossed their roles.

A pen that tells of mimes,
Who plotted with silly rhymes.
Cakes that spilt and spilled with glee,
In the land of cups of tea.

A page torn from a prank,
Where everyone forgot to thank.
The truth of the ice cream fights,
And hiding candy in the nights.

Echoing Laughter of Yesteryears

In the attic, echoes play,
Of laughter that won't fade away.
A jump rope that tells a tale,
Of treasure maps and fuzzy snails.

The old guitar rests in glee,
It still strums tunes of jubilee.
Ghosts of giggles roam the floor,
In every nook, they seek for more.

A rubber chicken on the wall,
Remembers when it caused a fall.
With wobbly chairs and sliding doors,
It sings of family fun galores.

Beneath the beams, the chortles bloom,
In every corner, bits of zoom.
Stories intertwined like threads,
In the laughter where fun spreads.

Muffled Footsteps in the Hallway

Muffled steps in the night air,
Sneaky squirrels look everywhere.
Tippy-toeing on the floor,
Listening for old tales in store.

A shadow darts around the bend,
Probably a sock's lifelong friend.
Each creak brings a chuckle near,
As giggles linger with no fear.

The cat leaps high with a twitch,
To catch the tales that seem to glitch.
Invisible pranks are everywhere,
Images of the playful air.

A book that talks of pies gone wrong,
And mischief that lasts all night long.
As whispers guide the feet to roam,
A silly dance in every home.

Echoes of Laughter in the Hallway

In the hallway, laughter's bound,
A rubber chicken, lost and found.
Dancing shadows, here they prance,
As dust bunnies join the silly dance.

The cat's a jester, with a hat,
Chasing mice that sound like chat.
Where socks are mismatched, glee's the game,
Oh, what fun, to join the fame!

The walls are whispering their delight,
With giggles echoing into the night.
A friendly ghost just passed on through,
Winking at all that we pursue.

Each step we take, a memory bred,
In goofy tales where laughter's fed.
With every creak, a joke declared,
This is the place where joy is shared.

Stories Told Through Cracks in the Ceiling

Listen close, the ceiling cracks,
Hold tales of squirrels and their snacks.
A nighttime chat with the moon so bright,
While shadows make up stories at night.

A spider spins a story thread,
About the times we laughed till we fled.
With popcorn ceiling, kernels of fun,
No tale is done, till we've begun.

The cracks, they giggle with delight,
While hiccuping lights join in the fight.
Of flying carpets and wobbly chairs,
Each tale we share—who really cares?

So peek above, and you might find,
Some funny tales left far behind.
The echoes linger, soft and true,
With every crack a joke anew.

The Gallery of Forgotten Wishes

In one corner, a wish to fly,
Stuck beneath a pizza pie.
Another yearning, for a pet bat,
Captured in a dusty hat.

The gallery glows in shades of fun,
Where dreams collide, and laughter's spun.
An old stuffed bear, with a silly grin,
Wishes to dance, let the fun begin!

A hidden wish for blueberry pie,
Hangs beside a pair of shoes, oh my!
Each dusty frame, a tale untold,
Where humor spills like pot of gold.

With every glance, a chuckle spills,
In ticklish air, the heart fulfills.
Forgotten wishes on the wall,
Remind us once, we had it all.

Beneath the Eaves

Beneath the eaves, the secrets keep,
Of raccoons that giggle and never sleep.
They hide and seek with empty cans,
Dancing on the porch in silly pants.

The birds drop jokes, and the bugs all cheer,
While windy whispers draw us near.
The grumpy old owl rolls his eyes,
At the punchlines flapping through the skies.

Across the beams, a parrot shouts,
Words like confetti, laughing routes.
A cozy spot for jesters to meet,
Where chuckles echo, oh so sweet.

With every bump, a comedy stands,
Beneath the eaves, where laughter lands.
So come and play, join the spree,
This is where the fun flows free!

Voices Resound

Voices resound, like bubbles in air,
Silly stories linger everywhere.
A pickle jar becomes a throne,
Where grand tales of lettuce are sown.

The toaster chimes a merry tune,
While socks sing softly to the moon.
Echoes of giggles twirl about,
In corners where fun has no doubt.

With each creak of the wooden floor,
A puppet shows behind the door.
Whispers of wonder from a child's heart,
In every room, it plays its part.

So gather around, let laughter out,
With every tale, let joy sprout.
Voices resound in delightful play,
Chasing the dreariness away!

The Key to Unwritten Tales

In the attic, dust bunnies roam,
Each corner holds a tale unknown.
A squeaky chair whispers secrets sweet,
While old boots dance, tapping their feet.

A wardrobe grins, with moths inside,
Hiding treasures, a comical ride.
The diary giggles, its pages turned,
With footnotes where all the fun is learned.

A cat strolls by, with stories to tell,
Of feasts and naps, oh what a swell!
Every shadow has a quirky spree,
Each dark corner chuckles back at me.

Between the Cracks of Existence

In a chair that creaks like an old man,
I find tales of a dustpan's plan.
Forks and spoons with stories to share,
Fossils of dinners caught unaware.

The floorboards squeak like they just can't wait,
To spill the beans on the dinner plate.
A sock hiccups, lost under the bed,
While curtains gossip about what's been said.

A broomstick dreams of flying high,
With all the debris that passes by.
As laughter cracks each wooden beam,
We tiptoe through this funny, funny dream.

Fragments Carved in Wood

A table, scratched, holds memories near,
With juice stains from the squeezer of cheer.
Chairs with character, chipped at the seams,
Crack up at jokes whispered in dreams.

A wooden spoon claps in the drawer,
Claiming the title of kitchen's lore.
Laughter echoes among the pots,
As the spatula flirts with all it's got.

The shelf wears dust like a fancy hat,
While books laugh out loud at a silly chat.
These fragments of timber, stories retold,
Paint a picture of a life so bold.

The Ghosts of Family Reunions

At Grandma's house, the stories are rife,
With echoes of laughter and the chaos of life.
Uncle Joe's socks, mismatched and bright,
Dancing in tales of a magical night.

Cousins play hide and seek, what a thrill,
In cupboards where grandpa's old boots spill.
Antics and tales of youthful delight,
Each face holds a grin that's broad and bright.

The dining table groans under the weight,
Of mishaps that set off a chain of fate.
And as stories loop, like a vintage tune,
Ghosts of laughter fill the room under the moon.

Interludes of Solace in the Corners

In the nook, dust bunnies plot,
Whispering tales, oh, what a lot.
The cat joins in with a lazy yawn,
As the clock ticks on, daytime's gone.

In the shadows, socks start to pair,
Odd ones dancing without a care.
Chairs creak secrets from days of yore,
While coffee spills tales on the floor.

Books stacked high, stories collide,
And the goldfish gossips about the tide.
Echoes of laughter bounce through the walls,
Inviting all to the merry brawls.

By the window, sunlight peeks,
Catching mischief in its streaks.
Every corner a laughter trap,
In this home, not a single nap.

The Gallery of Wandering Spirits

In the hall, echoes take a stroll,
Framed in laughter, a cheeky shoal.
Ghosts with jokes play hide and seek,
Tickling the cat, what a cheek!

Paintings wink as shadows play,
Each stroke a secret of yesterday.
Laughter drips from the ceiling high,
While a chair whispers, 'Here's my pie!'

The rug giggles underfoot,
As slippers dance, what a hoot!
Mismatched socks waltz by my side,
With giggles echoing, there's no pride.

In this display of silly sights,
Phantoms prance in neon lights.
Every corner a chuckle gears,
With wandering spirits, joy appears.

Fractals of Moments Past

Memories spin like tops on the floor,
Each one a laugh, a festive roar.
Grandma's casserole, a dubious treat,
Kitchen concoctions that can't be beat.

Photographs freeze their grinning charm,
Caught in antics, no cause for alarm.
A cat in a hat, a dog in boots,
Each captured smile, a riotous hoot!

Tickles of time in every thread,
Stories uncovered once they're spread.
In the fabric of life, colors clash,
Creating a tapestry, a playful splash.

Through fractals of moments, laughter rings,
Old tales sprout like comical springs.
In a whirl, the past won't fade,
For joy has a way to masquerade.

Chronicles of the Porch Swing

Swinging gently, whispers abound,
As crickets play their nighttime sound.
Each creak of wood tells a joke,
When the moon grins, and shadows poke.

A cup of tea spills over the rail,
As squirrels gather to share their tale.
With each kick, the cosmos sways,
Revealing the absurd side of days.

Grandpa chuckles, sharing a yarn,
While fireflies buzz with a hint of charm.
Every glance across the yard,
Turns a moment into a card!

Stories twirl in the evening air,
As we toss laughs without a care.
On the swing, we find our groove,
In chronicles of joy, we move.

Windows that Capture Time

Windows wide, the views so grand,
Catching tales from every hand.
Old man snorts, his bedtime snore,
Echoes of battles fought before.

Till glassy panes take on a glow,
Reflecting all the laughs we know.
Cats parade and dogs will prance,
While shadows join the evening dance.

Time floats like balloons in June,
Bouncing, bouncing, to a tune.
Catch a glimpse, then watch it flee,
Memories wave, "Come play with me!"

The Forgotten Room's Lament

In the corner, dust bunnies sigh,
Cobwebs weave their tales awry.
"What's that smell?" asks the curious cat,
While old shoes grumble, "Not where we sat!"

Books stacked high, they moan and groan,
Whispering secrets of the unknown.
A sock or two, they don't belong,
Sing to the wall in a faded song.

The door creaks, and what? A scare!
The ghost of laundry, unwashed despair.
With giggles masking the room's pitfall,
Stories keep rising, to have a ball!

Bowls of Stories and Dreams

Bowls stacked high, with tales galore,
Filled with giggles, never a bore.
Each spoonful stirs a laugh or two,
Like grandpa's jokes that still feel new.

Mixing memories, sweet and sour,
Tastes of laughter, hour by hour.
Be careful though, don't spill your dream,
Or you might find, it's not what it seems!

A pinch of whimsy, a dash of fun,
In every bowl, tales weigh a ton.
So gather 'round, dear friends and foes,
Let's fill our hearts till joy overflows!

Where Time Bends in the Hall

In the hall, time dances slow,
Bending light, a wild show.
Tick-tock says the old clock's voice,
But giggles scream, "You've no choice!"

Pictures grin and sneak a peek,
Watching antics, week by week.
The rug rolls up, the chairs all laugh,
As kids skip by, their own half-staff.

Pasting moments to the wall,
Each footstep echoes, a bouncing ball.
Stories spin on invisible strings,
Where laughter flies and joy still sings.

The Chime of a Greeting

Knock knock on the door, who is it this time?
A squirrel with a hat, claiming he's prime.
He dances on the porch, a sight to behold,
While my cat rolls her eyes, feeling quite bold.

The welcome mat shouts with a wink and a grin,
Inviting the chaos that's sure to begin.
The mailman slips on a banana peel,
And a parrot squawks gossip, it's all so surreal.

Inside the kitchen, pies fly through the air,
Baking disasters—oh, what a flare!
Grandma insists laughter's the best kind of cream,
While the dog steals the cakes, he's living the dream.

So here's to the whims, the chuckles, the cheer,
To the shenanigans we hold oh so dear.
In a place full of laughter where friends gather round,
Every corner echoes with joy that's profound.

Dreams in Dust and Shadows

Underneath the bed, there's a monster named Fred,
Telling jokes to the socks, as they quietly tread.
He guffaws at the dust bunnies, all gathered in pack,
While the lamp rolls its eyes, saying, 'Give it a whack!'

In the attic, a trunk full of treasures awaits,
With a jacket that squeaks and a hat that relates.
Whispers of pirates echo through old hats,
As the broom serves tea to forgetful old cats.

The shadows dance wildly, a flash of delight,
As the moon plays peek-a-boo, teasing goodnight.
A tinfoil spaceship takes flight off the shelf,
With aliens who giggle, just being themselves.

Each cobweb a tapestry, each creak a song,
In the corners of twilight, we all hum along.
Dreams twinkle like stars, in a house full of glee,
Where shadows share stories, roaming wild and free.

Tales Written in the Stars Above

At the tip of the roof, there's a storybook star,
Who claims that it's traveled both near and far.
It talks of adventures with elves on the run,
While arguing with moonbeams, oh what fun!

The chimney sweeps giggles as soot takes a leap,
While the clock strikes twelve, all the crickets peep.
A squirrel writes tales with his tail all a-flutter,
As the lightning bugs twinkle, it's pure story clutter.

Dream boats are floating on clouds made of cream,
With bubbles for sails, sailing up to a dream.
The wind tells a joke that flies high and low,
While a hedgehog plays banjo, putting on a show.

So let's raise a toast with cups filled with gleam,
To the stories above—each one a sweet dream!
For every twinkling star holds a giggle or two,
In the vast cosmic dance, there's always room for you.

The Breath of Time in Every Room

In the kitchen, a pot starts to dance,
While the fridge hums a tune, given half a chance.
Spatulas gossip with the shining plates,
As flour clouds settle on their dinner dates.

The living room's couch tells tales of naps,
Socks get lost in the cushions like crafty chaps.
A lamp winks knowingly, casting its light,
On secrets that giggle in the dark of night.

Upstairs, the shower sings off-key songs,
While the toilet whispers, 'Hey, take your longs!'
Mirrors reflect laughter, so vividly bright,
As toothpaste and brushes engage in a fight.

Down in the cellar, old boxes conspire,
With dusty old toys that once had a fire.
Each corner is filled with echoes of cheer,
Where laughter and echoes always draw near.

Requiem for a Faded Memory

An old shoe sighs from the corner of gloom,
Pinching the air with a musty perfume.
Once it ran races, now it lies still,
Dreaming of places on a forgotten hill.

A picture frame crumbles, its glass all askew,
Smiling at moments it once vividly knew.
Laughs once erupted from faces so bright,
Now trapped in the twilight of longing and light.

The clock ticks slowly, a jester's old jest,
While dust bunnies giggle, snug in their nest.
A book with torn pages whispers of love,
But finds itself longing for moments above.

In the attic, old memories prance and play,
As shadows dance gently, in their own way.
With laughter that echoes through time's gentle bend,
Each faded remembrance finds joy in the end.

Conversations with the Midnight Moon

The moon peeks in through a window wide,
Gathering secrets that shadows confide.
Whispers of dreams drift on soft midnight air,
As the cat chuckles, perched high on a chair.

Stars hold a council, all twinkling with glee,
Imagining worlds that we cannot see.
The floor creaks in delight, sharing tales of the past,
While the fridge claims to keep memories fast.

Pillows become ships sailing night's gentle sea,
Navigating thoughts, wild and fancy-free.
Lamps flicker in rhythm, a soft serenade,
While dust motes are dancers, in moonlight arrayed.

As the night stretches, laughter blends with dreams,
In this cosmic chatter, nothing is as it seems.
Each creak of the floor knows a joke or a pun,
In the realm of the night, we all join for fun.

Fleeting Shadows of Childhood

Under the bed where monsters still play,
Old toys reminisce of their glory days.
A teddy bear nods, wearing a grin,
While the army men plot their revolt from within.

The swings swing softly in the night breeze,
Whispering secrets among rustling leaves.
Jump ropes recount tales of hopscotch and cheer,
Reminded of laughter that once filled the year.

In the garden, gnomes host a picnic of fun,
Sipping on dew drops beneath the bright sun.
The treehouse is buzzing with giggles and screams,
Where every young dreamer dares to dream dreams.

Footsteps echo softly on paths made of stone,
Leaving shadows of memories, all their own.
Time tiptoes out, never wanting to stay,
As fleeting shadows dance toward the end of the day.

Whispers in the Walls

In the corner, a mouse did prance,
He's got some tales, would you give them a chance?
Whispers echo, oh what a delight,
Calling out secrets, deep in the night.

The wallpaper giggles, it knows all the news,
Of socks gone missing and wild, silly shoes.
Chandeliers chuckle, shining their light,
Keeping the stories that take flight at night.

Old pipes may rattle, with laughter unseen,
Sharing their thoughts on the house's routine.
Every crack and creak has a tale to unfold,
Of midnight feasts and praises retold.

So listen closely, to the chirps and the hums,
For the walls are alive, where laughter comes from.
With each little whisper, a story's renown,
In this lively abode, there's never a frown.

Echoes of Forgotten Rooms

In the attic, dust bunnies hold a ball,
They twirl and they spin, they're having a call.
Old dolls gossip and clatter their eyes,
With tales of their youth, oh how time flies!

Down in the basement, the shadows all dance,
As boxes exchange their most curious glance.
Regrets are tickled by an old rubber band,
Lost socks are debating who's in command.

A chair creaks softly, it's had quite a life,
With stories of family, joy, and some strife.
Echoes of laughter spill from each space,
Filling the rooms with warmth and with grace.

Silly echoes of parties, of foot-stomping fun,
Remind us that life is not done until one.
With whispers and chuckles sewn into the seams,
The house holds a treasure of whimsical dreams.

The Secrets Beneath the Floorboards

Underneath where the carpet lies thick,
Lurks a family of ants, they're planning a trick.
With tiny conspiracies, they pave out the way,
For crumbs left behind from yesterday's play.

The old floorboards creak with glee in the dark,
As they share little secrets, famous and stark.
Once a cat's hideout, now a fortress of fun,
Where whispers of shenanigans overrun.

In the hinges, you'll find stories of doors,
That open with laughter and close with their roars.
Every squeaky plank has a joke in its core,
Reminiscing the laughter that danced on the floor.

With a smack of the wall, like an old friend's embrace,
These secrets are waiting, they fill up the space.
So tap with your foot, give a playful old stomp,
Join in the revels that make the heart thump.

Windows to Lost Memories

Through the glass, the world shows its face,
Where the sun draws a smile, the clouds run a race.
Each frame holds a moment, a laugh, or a tear,
A window to stories we hold ever dear.

The curtains are dancing, swaying in glee,
Catching whispers of neighbors, oh what could they be?
In their folds lie the echoes of laughter and dreams,
A theatre of life, bright as sunlight beams.

Raindrops are storytellers, pattering fast,
As windows recount tales of summers long past.
With splashes of chalk on a sidewalk out there,
Each streak of color, a memory rare.

So draw back the drapes, let the world come alive,
For each pane is a portal that helps us survive.
In the sill, we gather our joys and our woe,
Discovering life through the glass's soft glow.

Hidden Passages of Emotion

In corners where laughter hides,
A sock puppet seeks some pride.
The cat knows all the secrets here,
Whispering tales for those who hear.

Underneath the worn-out stairs,
A toadstool kingdom, few compares.
With giggles spilling like a tea,
Fairy tales from the pantry tree.

The closet doors, a space for fun,
Where ghostly pranks have just begun.
They trip and stumble, laugh in fright,
Amidst the shadows, pure delight.

So gather round, let stories fly,
With every blink, a sweet surprise.
In this realm, the laughter grows,
Behind our walls, where joy just flows.

Stories Etched in Stone

On the patio, a gnome sits still,
With eyes that mimic every thrill.
His tales of mulch and hidden earth,
Bring giggles forth, a lawn's rebirth.

The garden path, a winding tale,
Where bees and blooms both dance and wail.
Every petal, a word so bright,
Weaving mishaps from day to night.

In the fountain, tiny splashes play,
As frogs recite, come join the fray.
A sprinkle here, a chuckle there,
In the backyard, magic's in the air.

So pause and wink at what you see,
For laughter lives in mystery.
With every stone, a verse can bloom,
In sunny nooks, or twilight's gloom.

Lullabies of the Long Forgotten

Beneath the bed, a monster snores,
While teddy bears conspire for scores.
In the land where dust bunnies leap,
They weave sweet dreams for us to keep.

The moonlight spills through curtains thin,
As bedtime creatures start their spin.
With mischievous eyes and wiggly toes,
They dance and giggle, nobody knows!

Grandpa's chair holds stories grim,
Of pirates lost on the ocean's whim.
With eye patches and a wooden leg,
He croaks, "Ahoy!" until they beg.

So curl up tight as the night unfolds,
Where every whisper a tale retolds.
In shadows cast by midnight's light,
Lullabies spring from fanciful fright.

The Window's Watchful Gaze

Through panes of glass, the laughter flows,
As chatty birds share gossip, who knows?
With every raindrop, a joke is shared,
Each puddle a stage, each laugh declared.

Silly shadows prance on the wall,
As the couch gets ready for a fall.
The curtains sway with a knowing grin,
As silliness peeks from deep within.

Across the street, the neighbors plot,
A pie-eating contest, oh what a lot!
The squirrels cheer with tiny claps,
As wins and losses stir the naps.

So lean in close, let stories ignite,
From window views, the world feels right.
In every glance, a tale unfurled,
Through laughter's lens, we see the world.

A Nest of Words Beneath Stars

Under the roof, tales tumble low,
Whispers and giggles, in soft undertow.
Stories of socks that mysteriously flee,
And how the cat stole the last cup of tea.

Cushions hold secrets, the couch knows too,
Of grandpa's wild tales, and Aunt Sue's shoe.
From shadows emerge giggles of glee,
As spacemen and pirates dance wild and free.

The walls are all ears, they've heard it all,
From epic fails to the time they played ball.
With popcorn in hand, we cheer and we jest,
In this nest of words, we feel truly blessed.

Beneath the stars, the stories ignite,
Laughter echoes sweetly, a pure delight.
Every line a puzzle, a riddle to find,
In the nest of words, we leave doubts behind.

The Kitchen Table of Remembrance

Gather 'round the table, where crumbs can tell,
Of batter-fueled battles and who cooked well.
The fork's a knight, the spoon's a brave maid,
Together they'll save the last slice we made.

'Member when breakfast was deemed a disaster?
The pancakes stuck fast, a sticky grandmaster!
Maple syrup rivers ran wild on the floor,
And Uncle Joe slipped—what a laugh, oh what lore!

The coffee pot gossips, in a brew so strong,
It remembers the laughter, the banter, the song.
Each spoonful of chaos, a taste we'll embrace,
In the kitchen of memories, we find our true place.

When we lift our mugs high, to the stories we share,
Every clink is a cheer, a moment laid bare.
At the kitchen table, where time takes its flight,
In each meal, a memory, a warm, sweet delight.

Patterns of Life on the Rugs

On colorful carpets, adventures unfold,
From battles of toys to missions so bold.
There's a race with a vacuum, who'll win? Who knows?
And the dust bunnies cheer for their buddy who glows.

Checkered designs hold the feet of the past,
With tales of spilled juice and cookies amassed.
The patterns are puzzle pieces, woven with cheer,
Filled with the laughter of everyone here.

A rug in the corner tells tales of a cat,
Who once thought a feather was far more than that.
With pawprints and giggles, it wears every stain,
A reminder of fun, of joy, and of pain.

As we tiptoe on stories that dance 'neath our feet,
We find life is patterned in laughter and heat.
With each playful step, we mosaic our way,
On these vibrant rugs, we'll forever stay.

Where Yesterdays Come to Visit

In the corner of time, memories smile,
They drop by for tea, linger for a while.
Old photos with mischief dance on the wall,
Where yesterdays gather, they catch us in thrall.

The clocks tick with laughter, seconds tick-tock,
As we share all the tales that make moments rock.
Yesterday's mishaps are today's best jokes,
Like when Dad wore socks with the wildest of cloaks.

Stories spill over like a pot on the stove,
With each little spill, there's more love to prove.
The silliness echoes, as joy finds its way,
Where yesterdays come knocking, in play after play.

Together we chuckle, as old tales revive,
In the warmth of the present, our memories thrive.
A gathering of laughter, the smiles are so wide,
Where yesterdays visit, forever our guide.

Whispers on the Windswept Porch

The old rocking chair creaks and groans,
Its tales of mischief, it gladly moans.
A cat sneezes loud, gives everyone a start,
While squirrels hold meetings with a nutty heart.

The neighbor's dog thinks he runs the show,
He howls at the moon like he's in a row.
Our giggles chase shadows, they slip and they slide,
As secrets escape like a well-aimed slide.

Here comes the postman, a package in hand,
Wrapped in bright colors, like he's in a band.
But inside? Just socks, a very odd gift,
We laugh 'til we cry, it's a perfect rift.

As the sun sets low and the stars interlace,
We whisper our wishes, each one a wild chase.
The house has its quirks, yet we love it so,
With whispers of laughter that always will flow.

Tales Tucked Behind Closed Doors

Behind every door lies a fragrant mess,
Of mismatched socks and a bit of distress.
A splash of paint, a cereal box tower,
Where yesterday's dinner still does have power.

In the attic, a squirrel made quite the scene,
His acorn collection, a sight rarely seen.
With hiccups and hoots, he scurries about,
While we peep through the cracks, giggling, no doubt.

Grandpa's tales of woe are hardly a bore,
About a lost shoe and the neighbor next door.
We howled as he spoke of a runaway duck,
Who crashed at the party, oh, what a pluck!

In this house of chaos, we find endless joy,
With stories of shoes, and a large rubber toy.
Though secrets may hide, and laughter escapes,
Behind every door, there's a world full of shapes.

The Gables that See It All

The gables on high, they giggle and stare,
At antics below with a whimsical flair.
A rain cloud surprised us, it drenched the whole crew,
Now everyone's dancing like mermaids in blue.

Up in the rafters, a raccoon once dined,
With snacks from the pantry, a feast so well-timed.
We threw him a party, but he ran away,
Leaving crumbs as evidence of his big play.

The windows, they whisper of cozy warm nights,
With stories that flicker like firefly lights.
A photo of Grandma, with her pet parakeet,
Who taught all the kids how to wiggle their feet.

And so in this place, where the walls seem to hum,
We gather our tales, and the laughter will come.
With gables that see, and hearts that are free,
In this playful world, we find our decree.

Hushed Silences of the Dormitory

In the corners, secrets quietly grow,
With whispers of dreams in the soft yellow glow.
A sock on the ceiling? Who tossed it up there?
We speculate wildly, with giggles to share.

Loud snores erupt like a mischievous tune,
While shadows creep softly beneath the full moon.
A midnight snack raid turns into a race,
As pillows go flying, oh, what a place!

The clock ticks away, each minute a tease,
As we pull off pranks, with slackened knees.
We hide under blankets, stifling our screams,
With visions of broccoli ruining our dreams.

In this hall of giggles, we forge our own fate,
With laughter and stories that always await.
Hushed are the sunsets, yet alive is the night,
In our dormitory, we find pure delight.

Shadows in the Attic

In the attic, dust bunnies play,
Chasing shadows, they leap and sway.
Old boxes laugh, they have their say,
Whispers of laughter, lost in the fray.

A trunk sings tunes of a pirate's plight,
A broomstick flies off into the night.
Pictures of things that just aren't quite right,
As ghosts in pajamas prepare for a fright.

Sock puppets chat, with stories outdated,
While knitting needles plot, quite elated.
The cat's in the corner, utterly baffled,
By tales of the past that have left him frazzled.

In the attic, the oddities gleam,
When daylight fades, they dare to dream.
With laughter and giggles, they craft their scheme,
A tale of the odd, or so it would seem.

Tales from the Hearth

By the fire, the flames sing bright,
Marshmallows dance in a sugary flight.
A potbellied stove tells of a night,
When spoons and forks found the perfect bite.

An apron whispers recipes of yore,
While the kettle teases, demanding more.
A pie's tantalizing, a tale to score,
Of secret ingredients, the family's lore.

The mantel is lined with trophies not grand,
For potato sack races, the family band.
Old photographs make silly demands,
As stories unfold, like grains of sand.

The laughter erupts, with a hearty cheer,
A floating ghost wishes it could draw near.
For tales from the hearth, so sweet and dear,
Are sprinkled with love, and maybe a beer.

Paintings of a Time Gone By

On the wall hangs a portrait with a grin,
It winks at the passerby, cheeky within.
With colors that danced and stories akin,
Of a party where everyone hoped to win.

In a hat that's too big, a dog on a chair,
Napping through nonsense, without a care.
The flowers are giggling, the sunlight's glare,
Painting memories that float in the air.

Each canvas a door to the past's little quirks,
Where cats argue politics, and nobody smirks.
Dancers on tables with fancy foot perks,
Their timeless fun, just how history works.

From laughter to silence, each brushstroke tells,
Of moments that bubble like wild, jolly spells.
In the frames of the house, a magic dispels,
Alive with the joy that precisely compels.

The Portrait that Spoke

In a frame on the wall, a character stirs,
With gossip and giggles in fanciful blurs.
A mustached chap who jovially purrs,
He spins tales of llamas and silly slurs.

He talks of old tea parties gone awry,
With cupcakes that launched into the sky.
His monocle glinting, an artful spy,
On secrets of pastries that even cakes sigh.

When visitors come, he whispers with flair,
"Have you heard of the duck who cut his own hair?"
With an eloquent smirk, he poses a dare,
To craft outrageous stories beyond compare.

So listen intently when he's in the room,
For laughter and whimsy shall surely boom.
The portrait that speaks, dispelling the gloom,
With tales so absurd, it's like a costume.

Reflections of Lives Once Lived

In the mirror, a ghost winks back,
Telling tales of mischief, what a knack!
Did Grandma really dance on the roof?
Or is that just a silly family spoof?

The parrot squawks with gossip grand,
Did Uncle Joe bring that pie to hand?
A laugh erupts from the kitchen's side,
As Aunt Sue claims she's the baker of pride.

Underneath the stairs, a secret drawer,
Holds love notes and socks we can't ignore.
Who was that player with charm so sweet?
We giggle and laugh at their clumsy feat.

With each crack in the floor, a memory twirls,
Of ice cream fights with messy swirls.
We chase the past like a game of tag,
As stories unfold in a hearty brag.

Ancestral Stories in the Attic

Up in the attic, dust and cheer,
An old trunk creaks, full of yesteryear.
A pirate hat and a feathered quill,
What's next? A time machine to thrill?

Grandpa's circuit board, what was that for?
He swore he could fly, just through the door.
And Aunt May's gown, with sequins all bright,
Portrayed her as disco queen, dance all night!

We step on the beams, hear whispers of fun,
Of sandcastles built, all before the sun.
Each relic just begs for a story to tell,
And laughter erupts like a magical spell.

We sit in the dust, holding a yarn,
Of how Grandma coaxed out all the charm.
The attic's a portal, where mishaps unfold,
And legends live on, in this treasure of old.

Footsteps in Silent Halls

Footsteps echo, a ghostly parade,
But it's just the cat, in a daring escapade.
He leaps on the counter, gives quite the scare,
As we chase him down, no time to spare!

Each creak of the floorboards, a story unfolds,
Of silly dances and laughter bold.
Grandpa's slippers, a sight to behold,
As he trips every time, oh, the humor is gold!

In corners, old photos peer out with a grin,
As if teasing us with secrets within.
We laugh at the mustaches, the hair dos so high,
And wonder how fashion ever flew by!

The empty halls feel alive today,
With memories wandering, and games in play.
We share all the tales that echo their call,
Ensuring their laughter still fills the hall.

Memories in Muffled Echo

In the whispering rooms, a tickle of jest,
Old chairs shake giggles, they know all the rest.
Did Dad really think he could eat all that pie?
With one bite he believed he could almost fly!

Photographs wink, with smiles long gone,
Captured in moments, as they carry on.
Grandma's sweater, with colors so bright,
Holds the warmth of hugs, igniting delight.

And on rainy days, the stories begin,
Of fanciful trips and the messes within.
Each shadowed corner holds laughter so clear,
Like a joyful tune that we always hear.

Muffled echoes bounce back, a riotous cheer,
Voices from the past feel so very near.
The house is alive with dreams and with lore,
Where giggles and tales forever soar.

Reflections in the Glass

In frames of wood, my face appears,
Smudged by laughter, smeared with cheers.
A wink and grin, a silly pose,
Reflections dance, who really knows?

The mirror chuckles, says, "Not fair!"
With toothpaste lies, and a purple hair.
I try to smile, it smirks back loud,
In the glass, a jester's crowd.

Lipstick trails and frowns galore,
A carnival held in my bathroom door.
I swear the soap just made a joke,
While shampoo waits, full of hope.

Each morning's show, a farce that's grand,
With laughter hidden in every strand.
So, if you see my silly stare,
Know the mirror's messing with my hair.

Whispers Between the Walls

The walls conspire, what a delight,
Telling tales throughout the night.
A rumble here, a giggle there,
Secrets shared in squeaks and air.

A ghostly shout from mom's old chair,
I swear it said, "Pull up a share!"
With every creak, a silly rhyme,
The house, it seems, loves fun at prime.

Windows wink, they've seen it all,
The antics that make silly calls.
A dance-off held on the wooden floor,
While the chimney giggles, wanting more.

In the attic, whispers grow bold,
Stories woven, some new, some old.
But all agree, with subtle glee,
This quirky house loves its spree.

Echoes of Forgotten Lullabies

In corners dark, a soft tune plays,
A melody from forgotten days.
The teddy bears sway and nod their heads,
While nursery rhymes fill time with threads.

Bouncing bunnies, teeny and spry,
Hopping on notes that flutter and fly.
A serenade of silly dreams,
With giggles woven in moonbeams.

The crib is now a stage for jokes,
Where socks conspire, and laughter pokes.
A lullaby with bursts of cheer,
Echoes softly, "Stay right here!"

Past bedside tales, forgotten lore,
A symphony of fun, it simply won't bore.
As echoes tease and gently sigh,
The night's a party, oh my, oh my!

The Attic's Secrets

Up in the attic, dust bunnies chat,
With old toys and hats, oh what of that?
They roll their eyes at yesterday's fights,
Gossiping 'bout the bold kite flights.

A lamp with a shade that's slightly awry,
Once lit up dreams beneath the sky.
It grins at the corners, whispering fun,
Together they reminisce about all they've done.

An old trunk creaks, might just break,
Holding secrets of every mistake.
But there's laughter too, and hats aplenty,
A giant mouse, who ain't so friendly.

So if you dare to climb up high,
Beware the sneakers that seem to sigh.
For in the attic's whimsical flight,
The secrets of laughter linger in light.

Reveries in the Quiet Corners

In the nook where dust bunnies play,
Old socks whisper secrets, they say.
A cat in a coat of dappled dreams,
Plots grand heists, or so it seems.

The chair talks back, can you believe?
It scoffs at gossip, tries to deceive.
A tickle here, a sneeze over there,
Makes me wonder if it's all fair.

Laughter echoes from picture frames,
As grumpy faces play silly games.
The rug rolls eyes at every mistake,
While curtains plot what pranks to make.

Beneath a light that hums and buzzes,
The fridge invents a life that fuzzes.
It croons love songs to a loaf of bread,
In dreams we dance, with crumbs to spread.

The Stairway of Lost Adventures

Each step creaks like an old-time tune,
Squeaking secrets beneath the moon.
I found a sock; it's missing its mate,
We think it wandered to a better fate.

Oh, what tales the banister could tell,
Of runaway toys and chips that fell.
It moans like a ghost with mischief planned,
As shadows waltz, by the floor's command.

A rubber duckie spied from the last flight,
Plotting parties with the winter's light.
Was that a giggle, or just a squeak?
Adventures await, though they may seem bleak.

Outdoors a garden, so grand and lush,
But here, mischief makes a merry rush.
Let's climb up high, let's roll back down,
For the stairs hold stories, as dreams go 'round.

Chronicles of Windows Long Closed

Behind the glass, where shadows play,
Old stories linger, in dusty display.
A gnome in a hat, with a wink and a grin,
Tells tales of chaos that no one can pin.

The latch creaks open; what's that I hear?
An opera sung by a forgotten deer!
A chorus of crickets, wild and free,
Turns classical woes into revelry.

Mothballs dance with a flair of disgrace,
While ghosts do the tango in their own space.
Each frame a portal to times that were grand,
With giggles and hiccups each time they stand.

So peek through the curtains, let whimsy unfurl,
When sunlight beams in, let laughter swirl.
In corners where dreams and reality meet,
You'll find nothing mundane, only joy bittersweet.

Ancestral Echoes in the Breeze

Whispers of my kin float on air,
With every gust, their tales lay bare.
Great Aunt Lila in her polka-dots,
Always claims she dodged all the plots.

Uncle Fred blames the cat for his shoe,
While Cousin Jane fought a ghost that just flew.
Their stories collide in a thrilling blend,
With laughter and sighs that never end.

The trees lean in, for they want to know,
What foolish antics will today's wind blow?
With roots in the ground, they all can relate,
To the pranks of the past that can never abate.

We sit and we chuckle, beams in our eyes,
As wisdom and folly become our prize.
In the breezy air, we find the delight,
In echoes of laughter, both day and night.

Shadows of Lament and Joy

In the attic, ghosts dance slow,
Swapping tales of long ago.
One's stuck in a polka dot dress,
Laughing hard, oh what a mess!

A cat who thinks he's quite the sage,
Grows wise with every turn of the page.
He purrs while fixing life's big blunder,
Telling secrets of love and thunder.

The walls hold whispers, both sad and sweet,
Of clumsy trips and fancy feet.
Happiness hides in the shadows thin,
In laughter lost, where tales begin.

So come find joy in the laughter's tears,
As memories twirl through the passing years.
Every giggle, a spark in the night,
Where shadows of both lament and delight.

Pockets of Time in the Telephone Nook

In the corner sits an old, rickety phone,
It rings with stories, never alone.
Who called last? Oh, a friend with a cat,
Whiskers curling, imagine that!

The chatter echoes, a sweet serenade,
A pocket of time where laughter's made.
Gossip of neighbors and boyfriend woes,
All spin together as the dial tone glows.

With every ring, a tale unfolds,
Of knitting mishaps and secrets bold.
Voices mix in a comical stew,
Who knew small talk could craft joy anew?

So wander by, hear the stories spun,
In the nook where the laughter runs.
Every call a slice of glee,
In pockets of time, come share with me!

Ceramics and Stories on the Shelf

On the shelf, a teapot grins wide,
Chirping gossip from the porcelain side.
A cup with a chip, oh what a chat!
It laughs, 'I'll spill the beans on that!'

A dog-shaped creamer with a cheeky bark,
Recalls the evenings that turned into dark.
Together they share quirks and quirks,
Of clumsy hosts with dance floor jerks.

The plates all giggle, forming a crew,
Telling tales of every spilled stew.
With every clatter, a memory calls,
In a symmetry of laughter, it enthralls.

So let them shine and tell their fun,
Ceramics and stories, oh what a run!
Each piece a marker of jest and cheer,
On the shelf, where giggles appear!

The Nooks that Nurture

In corners snug, where giggles bloom,
The nooks all pulse with vibrant zoom.
A hammock swings with stories to weave,
Where dreams and dreams together cleave.

A beanbag sighs, it's seen it all,
From whispered secrets to friendship's call.
We share our worries, then burst with glee,
Nurtured by comfort, so wild and free.

A window seat where the sunbeams play,
Catching laughs as they drift away.
Every nook's a world, with tales to boast,
Of silly mishaps and laughter's toast.

So snuggle in, let the giggles ignite,
These nooks that nurture bring pure delight.
In fun-filled corners, let's spin our lore,
Where every laugh opens a new door!

Battle Scars of a Humble Abode

There's a hole in the wall, it tells me quite bold,
A racquetball game that went out of control.
A family of mice, looking quite spry,
They've claimed all my cheese, I just sit here and sigh.

The fridge keeps on humming a tune of its own,
While the cat plots a coup from his cushiony throne.
Each battle that's fought, with laughter we share,
In this charming estate where we declare, beware!

The floorboards creak tales of decades gone by,
Of socks left unpaired and a dinner gone dry.
There's a dent on the couch where the dad used to nap,
His snores shook the windows; what a wild mishap!

So raise up a toast to this lovely old place,
With antics unending and laughter's embrace.
Each scar tells a story, a giggle or two,
Here's to the chaos that makes life feel new!

Harmony in the Raccoon's Nest

There's a raccoon that visits, he thinks he's so sly,
He waltzes on rooftops, oh how he can fly!
Umbrellas and garbage cans, such a grand show,
He juggles with peanut butter, "Oh look at me go!"

At night we'll discuss all the snacks he can steal,
A master of mischief with fervor and zeal.
He's taken a shine to my shiny new bin,
And I'm left with the crumbs while he snickers a grin.

With friends in the attic, a squirrel on the phone,
They plot out their schemes in a language unknown.
Count how many donuts can fit in one paw,
Their giggles make legends—"Did you see that great score?"

In this grand band of ruffians, laughter's the key,
In every corner, a giggle set free.
As the sun sinks away, we dance 'neath the trees,
For the raccoon's great tales are the best kind of tease!

The Memories That Dwell Alongside

There's an old chair that sways with a squeak every time,
It tells tales of tea with laughter so prime.
With each little rock, it reveals silly pranks,
Like that time Auntie Marge fell into the tanks!

The walls hold the secrets of games late at night,
Of whispers and giggles and feigned frightful fright.
A tapestry woven with love and delight,
In corners where echoes of joy take their flight.

There's a shelf full of trinkets, a wonderland mix,
Old rubber chickens and some colorful sticks.
A conch from the beach, a sock that once flew,
They all got a story that's waiting for you.

So dance with the shadows that flicker and play,
Where memories gather and leap in array.
With each little stumble and giggle-filled cheer,
This place binds us close, oh so perfectly dear!

Knots of Time in Every Room

In the bathroom, a sock from the laundry does flop,
It's tangled with time and it just won't stop.
The faucets will chatter, they gossip and brag,
About soap opera antics, like a dramatic old rag.

In the kitchen, the timer sings a curious tune,
As the kettle does jiggle like it's dancing to June.
A blender that hums of adventures it knows,
Of smoothies gone wild and spilled marinara flows.

The bedroom holds whispers of dreams gone astray,
Pillow fights laughter, as night turns to day.
Beneath fluffy blankets where memories sprout,
Are secrets of daydreams we can't live without.

And so every corner has stories to tell,
Of laughter and chaos; we've managed quite well.
In knots of our lives, in rooms thick with cheer,
This place is our canvas—let's paint it sincere!

Portraits of Lingering Echoes

In the hall, a sock still waits,
For its mate who always skates.
A whispered laugh, a creaky floor,
Echoes linger, wanting more.

A cat that thinks it owns the chair,
Meows at ghosts that aren't quite there.
A picture framed with glares so bright,
Winks at secrets, day and night.

Timeworn Tales from Every Corner

Beneath the stairs, a treasure chest,
Filled with junk—who'd have guessed?
A rubber duck from days gone by,
Croaks its tales, oh my, oh my!

The fridge hums stories, old and bold,
Of leftovers that refuse to mold.
Pickle jars that dance on shelves,
Wave at memories of younger selves.

Curtains that Conceal

Curtains twitch with a cheeky breeze,
Whispering secrets of the bees.
A half-drawn shade hides a winking cat,
Who thinks it's clever, imagine that!

Behind the fabric, the dust bunnies play,
Dancing about, they lead astray.
With giggles muffled in shadow's grasp,
Curtains know more than they can clasp.

The Resilient Walls

Walls wear laughter like a badge,
Holding stories of each scuffle and rage.
With cracks that laugh at every fall,
They know the fun, they've seen it all!

Each bump, a chuckle locked in time,
Whispers of mischief in rhyme and chime.
A tickle here, a poke right there,
Walls stand tall, with a wink and flair.

Faded Portraits and Ink-Stained Pages

Faded faces on the wall,
Mouths that whisper tales of brawl.
Ink-stained pages tell a jest,
History wearing a funny vest.

Grandpa danced in polka dots,
A cat that stole his favorite pots.
A letter written with a grin,
Who knew childhood was such a win!

The dog wore glasses, thought he was keen,
In every picture, a silly scene.
Mismatched socks on every chair,
Laughter echoes everywhere.

Old stories laid in jumbled stacks,
When ghosts prank, they never relax.
Life's too short for frowns and sighs,
In these pages, humor lies.

The Hearth's Hidden Narratives

The hearth crackles with a spark,
Whispers join the shadows dark.
Marshmallows fly across the room,
While laughter chases off the gloom.

A raccoon stole the whole pie,
Pointing claws as if to cry.
While everyone chased in a loop,
We found him dancing with the soup!

Chairs meant for the wise and bold,
Hold secrets shared and tales retold.
Every flame as sharp as jest,
Tickles the heart, it's the best quest.

Through the ash and charcoal gray,
Funny things never fade away.
The cracks may boast a thousand years,
They chuckle softly, bring back cheers.

Secrets Beneath the Floorboards

Underneath the wooden planks,
Mouse-sized stories, mighty pranks.
Beneath each creak, a tale unfolds,
Of treasure hunts and pirate golds.

A sock lost in a daring chase,
Waging war on a paper lace.
Every squeak gives way to cheer,
As giggles hide behind the ear.

Secrets squeak and peek from cracks,
Poking fun at all our quacks.
Jumping jests beneath our toes,
As we strut where laughter grows.

Oh, the noise they love to make,
Beneath our feet, the joy they stake.
Each step's a dance, a playful glide,
With stories tickling, they can't hide.

Lantern Light and Dusty Dreams

The lantern swings, a wobbly beam,
Catching giggles that brightly gleam.
Dust settles in a wavy swirl,
Where stories spin and laughter twirl.

Underneath its flickery glow,
Dreams prance 'round, both high and low.
A giraffe in pajamas, what a sight!
The night is young, let's hold on tight.

Whispers float like happy chants,
Playing hopscotch in their pants.
Dancing shadows take their flight,
In the soft embrace of night.

Every corner holds a whimsy,
Brighten stories with a frenzy.
In the lantern's warm embrace,
Laughter spreads all over the place.

www.ingramcontent.com/pod-product-compliance
Lightning Source LLC
Chambersburg PA
CBHW062110280426
43661CB00086B/435